Poetics

*The Foundations of Storytelling
and Dramatic Theory*

A Modern Translation

Adapted for the Contemporary Reader

Aristotle

Table of Contents

Preface - Message to the Reader

Rebuilding the Greatest Library in Human History

Thousands of years ago, the Library of Alexandria was the heart of global knowledge — a sanctuary where the wisdom of every known civilization was gathered and shared freely.

And then, it was lost.

Now, we're rebuilding it — and you are invited to join us.

At the Library of Alexandria, we've set out to make every book available to *every person on Earth* — not just in print, but in every language, every format, and for every reader.

Here's how we do it:

- **Deluxe Print Editions at True Printing Cost** - Order any book as a high-quality paperback, elegant hardcover, or stunning boxset — and only pay what it costs to print. No markups. No middlemen.

- **Unlimited Access to the Greatest Works** - Enjoy thousands of timeless classics — from Plato to Shakespeare to Tolstoy — in beautiful, modern eBook and audiobook editions. Read and listen without limits — for every reader, everywhere.

- **Modern Translations for Every Language & Dialect** - We're reimagining the classics in clear, accessible language — and translating them into every dialect imaginable. Everyone deserves to understand humanity's greatest ideas.

When you visit **LibraryofAlexandria.com**, you're not just accessing books — you're joining a global movement to restore, preserve, and share the wisdom of civilization.

Join us today at LibraryofAlexandria.com

Together, we'll ensure the light of human wisdom never fades again.

With gratitude,
The Modern Library of Alexandria Team

Visit:

www.libraryofalexandria.com

Or scan the code below:

1

Introduction

Ancient Greece was a civilization famous for its great contributions to philosophy, politics, art, and science. It thrived from the 8th century BCE until the Roman Empire started to decline. Greece's city-states, especially Athens, were the heart of culture and intellectual thought. This was the time when democracy began, impressive buildings like the Parthenon were built, and famous playwrights like Sophocles and Euripides produced their works. The Greeks' curiosity about the world around them laid the foundation for Western philosophy. Thinkers like Socrates, Plato, and later Aristotle, pushed the limits of what people understood about the world.

Greek society was deeply connected to theism, which focused on a large group of gods and goddesses who were believed to control every part of life. But this system did not prevent people from exploring new ideas. In fact, it coexisted with a growing interest in finding logical explanations for nature and human life. Intellectuals would often debate and discuss these ideas in public places like the Agora. Aristotle grew up in this dynamic environment, learning from earlier philosophers, and later challenging and expanding their ideas.

Aristotle's Life

Aristotle was born in 384 BCE in a small town called Stagira, located in northern Greece. His father, Nicomachus, was a doctor for King Amyntas of Macedon, and this allowed Aristotle to be around the Macedonian royal court from a young age. When his parents passed away, Aristotle was sent to Athens at the age of 17 to pursue his education. Athens was the center of intellectual life in Greece, and Aristotle joined Plato's Academy, which was the most respected school of the time. The Academy was a place where students discussed everything from ethics to science. Although Aristotle learned a lot from Plato, he did not always agree with him, especially when it came to metaphysics, which deals with the nature of reality.

After spending almost 20 years at the Academy, Aristotle left Athens around 347 BCE after Plato's death. He traveled around different cities in Greece, continuing to study and learn. In 343 BCE, he was invited to the court of King Philip II of Macedon, where he became the tutor of Philip's son, Alexander, who would later become known as Alexander the Great. Aristotle taught Alexander about philosophy, ethics, politics, and science. Aristotle's influence is visible in Alexander's leadership style, which showed respect for knowledge and strategic thinking.

After teaching Alexander, Aristotle returned to Athens in 335 BCE, where he opened his own school called the Lyceum. Unlike Plato's Academy, the Lyceum focused more on recording knowledge and observing nature. Aristotle and his students performed research, studied animals, and took notes on what they observed. The Lyceum became a major center of learning, and it rivaled Plato's Academy. This is also where Aristotle wrote many of his famous works.

Later in life, after the death of Alexander in 323 BCE, the political climate in Athens became difficult for Aristotle because of his connections to the Macedonian court. Accused of disrespecting the gods, Aristotle decided to leave Athens. He fled to Chalcis, where he passed away in 322 BCE. Even though he had to leave Athens, his legacy lived on through his many writings and the influence of his school, the Lyceum.

Aristotle's Impact on Western Thought

No figure looms larger over the development of Western philosophy and science than Aristotle. A student of Plato and tutor to Alexander the Great, he unified logic, ethics, politics, rhetoric, and metaphysics into a coherent system that shaped intellectual inquiry for centuries. Although his writings reflect the best knowledge of his era, they also reveal a distinctive way of understanding the world—one that balances observation with rigorous logical analysis. Over time, this method has profoundly influenced everything from political theory to modern scientific methodology.

Aristotle approached knowledge as an interconnected whole, seeing each field of study as a vital path toward truth. While many earlier thinkers focused on abstract concepts, he emphasized direct observation of the natural world. By systematically examining and classifying what he saw, Aristotle laid the groundwork for the empirical methods now central to modern science. Although our understanding of nature has evolved, his legacy endures in today's emphasis on evidence-based research.

Logic: The Foundation of Rational Inquiry

Often hailed as the "father of formal logic," Aristotle introduced a system of reasoning that shaped intellectual discourse for over two millennia. In works like the Organon, he analyzed how valid conclusions are drawn from premises and introduced syllogisms—deductive arguments that became standard tools in philosophy, theology, and science. Even contemporary logic, despite its modern mathematical and symbolic advancements, can trace many of its core principles back to Aristotle's pioneering analyses.

Metaphysics: Exploring the Nature of Reality

Aristotle's Metaphysics offered one of the earliest comprehensive explorations of existence at its most fundamental level. There, he described the nature of "being qua being" and introduced the concepts of potentiality and actuality to explain how things change and develop. These ideas deeply influenced medieval scholastics—both Christian and Islamic—who integrated Aristotelian reasoning into their theological frameworks. Today, discussions about consciousness, identity, and free will still reference these Aristotelian notions.

Ethics and the Pursuit of the Good Life

In the Nicomachean Ethics, Aristotle proposed that the ultimate aim of human life is eudaimonia, often translated as "happiness" or "flourishing." He argued that we achieve this through virtue, developed by cultivating good habits guided by reason. His famous Doctrine of the Mean asserts that moral virtue resides between two extremes—for instance, courage lies between recklessness and cowardice. This focus on character formation has profoundly shaped the tradition known as "virtue ethics," influencing modern debates on moral education, personal development, and what it means to live well.

Politics: The Role of the Individual in the City-State

Aristotle's practical approach to ethics naturally extended into political theory. In Politics, he explored various forms of government—monarchy, aristocracy, oligarchy, democracy—and weighed their merits and pitfalls. For Aristotle, a well-ordered polis (city-state) exists not merely for survival or trade but to enable its citizens to live virtuous, fulfilling lives. His conviction that ethics and politics are intertwined remains influential, informing contemporary discussions on citizenship, governance, and justice.

Rhetoric: The Art of Persuasion

In his treatise Rhetoric, Aristotle examined how persuasion works, detailing how arguments must appeal to ethos (credibility), pathos (emotion), and logos (logic). This clear framework for effective communication continues to guide public speakers, legal advocates, and writers. From ancient courtroom orations to modern political campaigns, Aristotelian rhetoric underpins many of the strategies people use to sway audiences and shape public opinion.

Beyond these core subjects, Aristotle made significant contributions to biology, physics, psychology, and aesthetics. In the Poetics, for example, he investigated why humans respond so powerfully to tragic drama, pioneering the concept of catharsis— the emotional release that audiences feel through art. Throughout the medieval period, thinkers like Thomas Aquinas integrated Aristotle's theories into Christian theology, while Islamic philosophers such as Avicenna and Averroes preserved, interpreted, and expanded upon his works.

Across centuries of reinterpretation and debate, Aristotle remains a living voice in contemporary thought. His insistence on systematically gathering evidence and connecting it to logical principles laid the foundation for what we now recognize as the scientific method. His inquiries into human flourishing, civic responsibility, and the nature of argument continue to spark discussion and inspire new research. From personal ethics to societal organization, Aristotle's ideas help us frame enduring questions about how best to live, learn, and understand reality.

In sum, Aristotle stands as a foundational pillar of Western thought. He bridged abstract theorizing and practical inquiry, bequeathing a vision of knowledge that values both reason and experience. From ethics and politics to science and art, his ideas have been woven into countless intellectual traditions. Even today, as we grapple with questions of morality, governance, and truth, we walk in the footsteps of an ancient thinker whose breadth of insight and depth of analysis continue to guide our pursuit of wisdom.

Final Thoughts

By preserving Aristotle's legacy, we protect the intellectual depth and rigor that defined his way of understanding the world. His systematic way of asking questions, his classification of knowledge, and his ethical theories are still relevant today, providing a model for critical thinking across many subjects. This preservation is important not just for philosophy students but for anyone interested in the foundations of human thought and the development of ideas that shape the world we live in.

One of the difficulties in studying Aristotle's work is that his ideas and language are complex. Translating these works into our modern language is a key step in making his profound insights easier for more people to understand. By putting his ideas into today's language, more readers can engage with his thoughts, even if they don't have a background in classical studies. Making Aristotle's work accessible means adapting them to modern ways of thinking without losing their original depth. This helps bridge the gap between ancient and modern readers, making sure Aristotle's work stays relevant.

Section 1

I will discuss poetry itself and its different types, noting the main features of each. I'll also look into how the plot should be structured to create a good poem, the number and type of parts a poem is made of, and other topics that are part of this study. Following the natural order, let's start with the most basic principles.

Epic poetry, tragedy, comedy, dithyrambic poetry, and music played on the flute or lyre, in most of their forms, are all ways of imitating. However, they differ from each other in three ways: the medium they use, the objects they imitate, and the method or style of imitation, which is different for each.

Just as some people use color and shape to imitate things, or others use their voice, in these arts, the imitation is done using rhythm, language, or harmony, either alone or in combination.

In flute and lyre music, for example, harmony and rhythm are used. In other similar arts, like playing the shepherd's pipe, the same is true. In dancing, rhythm is used without harmony. Dancing also imitates character, emotions, and actions through rhythmic movements.

There is another art that imitates only through language, and this can be in either prose or verse. The verse can use a single meter or combine different meters. This type of art doesn't have a specific name. For example, we don't have a general term for both the mimes of Sophron and Xenarchus, or for the Socratic dialogues, or for poems written in iambic or elegiac meter. People add the word "poet" or "maker" to the name of the meter and call them elegiac poets or epic poets, as though the verse form, not the imitation, makes someone a poet. Even if a treatise on medicine or science is written in verse, the author is still called a poet by custom. Yet Homer and Empedocles only share the same meter, so it would make more sense to call one a poet and the other a scientist. Using the same logic, if a poet used all meters in one work, like Chaeremon did in his "Centaur," which is a mix of all kinds of meters, we would still call him a poet.

Now that these distinctions are clear, we can see that some arts use all the means of rhythm, tune, and meter. This is true for dithyrambic and nomic poetry, as well as for tragedy and comedy. The difference is that in the first two, all these elements are used together, while in the latter, one may be used more than the others.

These are the differences between the arts in how they imitate.

Since the things being imitated are people in action, and people are either of a higher or lower moral type (because morality is based on goodness and badness), we must show people as better than they are, worse than they are, or as they really are. The same idea is used in painting. Polygnotus painted people as nobler than they are, Pauson painted them as less noble, and Dionysius painted them as they appear in real life.

It's clear that each form of imitation will show these differences and become its own type by imitating these different kinds of people. We can see these differences even in dancing, flute playing, and lyre playing. The same is true in language, whether in prose or verse without music. For example, Homer makes people better than they are, Cleophon shows them as they are, and Hegemon, the inventor of parodies, and Nicochares, the author of The Deiliad, portray people as worse than they are. The same applies to dithyrambs and nomes, where Timotheus and Philoxenus differ in how they represent their

Cyclopes. This difference also sets apart tragedy from comedy. Comedy tries to show people as worse, while tragedy shows them as better than they are in real life.

There is another difference in how these things can be imitated. With the same medium and the same objects, a poet can either narrate the story by speaking as another person, as Homer does, or by speaking in their own voice. Or, the poet can present all the characters as if they are living and acting in front of us.

So, as we said before, the three differences that separate artistic imitation are the medium, the objects, and the manner. From one perspective, Sophocles imitates in the same way as Homer because both show noble characters. From another perspective, Sophocles imitates in the same way as Aristophanes because both show people taking action. That's why some people say the word "drama" is used for such works, because they show action. For the same reason, the Dorians claim they invented both tragedy and comedy. The Megarians claim comedy started with them, saying it began under their democracy, and the Megarians of Sicily also claim it, noting that the poet Epicharmus, who lived before Chionides and Magnes, was from their land. Some Dorians in the Peloponnese also claim tragedy as their invention. In each case, they support their claims with language.

They say that the villages, which they call "komai," were where comedians went, as opposed to the Athenians who called them "demoi." Comedians, they say, weren't named after the word "komazein," which means "to revel," but because they wandered from village to village after being excluded from the city. They also say that the Dorian word for "to act" is "dran," while the Athenian word is "prattein."

Poetry seems to have developed from two natural causes. First, the instinct to imitate is built into humans from childhood. This instinct sets us apart from other animals because we are the most imitative creatures and learn our earliest lessons through imitation. We also naturally enjoy seeing things that are imitated. We can see proof of this in experience. We may feel disgusted by the sight of certain animals or dead bodies in real life, but we enjoy looking at them when they are accurately recreated in art. This is because learning brings us pleasure, not just to philosophers but to people in general, though to different degrees. This is why people enjoy seeing a likeness—when they see it, they recognize it and think, "Oh, that's him." If you've never seen the original, though, the pleasure won't come from the imitation itself but from the skill of the artist or some other factor like the colors used.

Imitation, then, is one of our natural instincts. Another is the instinct for harmony and rhythm, with meters clearly being sections of rhythm. People who had this natural gift developed it over time, using their talents to gradually create poetry from simple improvisations.

Poetry then split into two paths, depending on the character of the writers. The more serious poets imitated the actions of noble men, while those who were less serious imitated the actions of common people, first composing satires. The serious poets wrote hymns to the gods and praises of great men. We don't know of any satirical poets before Homer, but there were probably many. Starting with Homer, we can name examples, such as his Margites and similar works. The right meter for satire was also introduced here, which is why the meter is still called the iambic or lampooning meter, as it was used for mocking each other. The early poets were known for writing either heroic verse or mocking verse.

Just as Homer is the greatest of serious poets, combining dramatic form with excellent imitation, he was also the first to outline the basics of comedy by dramatizing the ridiculous instead of simply writing personal attacks. His Margites is to comedy what the Iliad and Odyssey are to tragedy. When tragedy and comedy came into existence, the two types of poets continued to follow their natural paths: the satirists became writers of comedy, and the epic poets were followed by tragedians since drama was a more advanced and higher form of art.

There is a question of whether tragedy has fully developed its proper forms, and whether it should be judged by itself or in relation to its audience. But either way, tragedy—like comedy—began with simple improvisations. Tragedy came from the authors of dithyrambs, and comedy from those who wrote phallic songs, which are still sung in some cities today. Tragedy developed slowly, with each new element building on the last. After many changes, it reached its natural form and stayed that way.

Aeschylus was the first to introduce a second actor. He reduced the role of the chorus and made dialogue the main part. Sophocles added a third actor and introduced scene painting. Tragedy also evolved from having a short plot to having a more complex one, and the rough language of early satyr plays gave way to the formal style of tragedy. The iambic meter replaced the trochaic tetrameter, which was originally used when the poetry was more like a satyr play and involved more dancing. Once dialogue became central, the iambic meter was naturally discovered because it is the meter that best suits speech. We can see this because everyday speech often falls into iambic rhythm, but rarely into hexameter unless we intentionally change our tone. The increase in the number of episodes or acts, and the other changes tradition tells us about, should be seen as already covered, since going into detail would be too long an explanation.

Comedy, as we've mentioned, is an imitation of characters of a lower type—not bad in the full sense of the word, but more like a funny kind of ugliness. It involves some kind of flaw or ugliness that doesn't cause pain or harm. For example, a comic mask may look ugly and twisted, but it doesn't suggest pain.

The changes that Tragedy went through and the people who made those changes are well known. However, Comedy doesn't have a history because it wasn't taken seriously at first. It wasn't until later that the Archon gave a poet permission to have a comic chorus; before that, the performers were volunteers. By the time specific comic poets came along, Comedy had already taken on its definite shape. We don't know who introduced masks or prologues or added more actors, or other similar details. The plot of Comedy, however, originally came from Sicily, and in Athens, Crates was the first to move away from the "iambic" or mocking form and created more general themes and plots.

Epic poetry is similar to Tragedy because it's also an imitation of characters of a higher type, written in verse. They differ because Epic poetry only uses one kind of meter and is told in a narrative form. Another difference is their length: Tragedy usually tries to fit within one day or slightly longer, while Epic poetry doesn't have time limits. This is a second difference, although in the early days, Tragedy had the same freedom as Epic poetry.

Some parts of Epic poetry and Tragedy are the same, while some are specific to Tragedy. So, if someone knows what makes a good or bad Tragedy, they'll also know about Epic poetry. Tragedy contains all the elements of an Epic poem, but Epic poems don't include all the elements of a Tragedy.

As for poetry written in hexameter verse, and for Comedy, we'll discuss those later. Let's now focus on Tragedy, starting by defining it again, based on what we've already said.

Tragedy is an imitation of an important and complete action that has a certain scale, using language that is decorated with artistic elements like rhythm, music, and verse in different parts of the play. It's presented through action, not storytelling, and it works to stir emotions like pity and fear, which then leads to a purging of these emotions. By "language decorated," I mean language that includes rhythm, music, and song. By "different parts," I mean that some parts use only verse, while others use song.

Since Tragedy shows people acting, the first thing it needs is the Spectacle, or what we see on stage. Next, it needs Song and Diction, which are the tools used to imitate. By "Diction," I mean the arrangement of words in a specific meter, and as for Song, everyone understands what that means.

Tragedy imitates an action, and action involves characters who have certain qualities of thought and character. These qualities are important because they define actions, and actions are what lead to success or failure. So, the Plot is an imitation of the action, and by "Plot," I mean the arrangement of events. By "Character," I mean the traits that let us describe the people in the play. "Thought" refers to when something is proven or a general truth is stated.

Every Tragedy must have six parts, which determine its quality: Plot, Character, Diction, Thought, Spectacle, and Song. Two of these are the medium of imitation, one is the method of imitation, and three are the objects of imitation. These six parts make up the complete list. Every play uses these elements; in fact, all plays have some Spectacle as well as Character, Plot, Diction, Song, and Thought.

Butthemostimportantpart of a Tragedy is thestructure of the incidents. Tragedy imitates actions, not people, and life is made up of actions. The purpose of life is a way of acting, not a quality of character. While

21

character defines qualities, happiness or unhappiness comes from actions. Therefore, Tragedy focuses on action, with character playing a secondary role. The events and the plot are the most important part of Tragedy because they represent the goal of the play, and the goal is the main thing. Without action, there can't be a Tragedy, but there can be one without character. Many modern poets fail to create good characters, and this is true of poets in general. It's the same with painting: the difference between Zeuxis and Polygnotus is that Polygnotus painted character well, while Zeuxis's style lacked moral qualities. Also, if you put together a series of speeches that show character and are well-written in terms of diction and thought, you still won't create the true tragic effect as well as you would with a play that has a strong plot and well-constructed events. Plus, the most powerful emotional elements in Tragedy, like Reversal of the Situation and Recognition scenes, are parts of the plot. A further point is that beginners in the art of writing often master diction and character portraits before they can construct a good plot. This is true for nearly all early poets.

So, the plot is the most important part of a Tragedy, almost like the soul of the play, while character comes second. You can see a similar example in painting: the most beautiful colors, if applied randomly, won't give as much pleasure as a simple outline drawn with chalk. In the same way, Tragedy imitates actions, and the people in it are there mainly to serve the action.

Next in importance is Thought, which is the ability to say what's possible and relevant in a given situation. In public speaking, this is the function of political or rhetorical art. The older poets made their characters speak like everyday people, while today's poets make them talk like rhetoricians. Character shows moral purpose by revealing what a person chooses or avoids. So, speeches that don't show this, or where the speaker doesn't make any choices, aren't revealing character. Thought, on the other hand, is present when something is proven or when a general idea is expressed.

Next in the list is Diction, which, as I've said before, is the expression of meaning through words. It's the same in both verse and prose.

Of the remaining elements, Song is the most important when it comes to artistic decoration.

The Spectacle has its own emotional appeal, but out of all the parts, it's the least artistic and least connected to the art of poetry. The power of Tragedy can be felt even without the performance and actors. Also, the creation of spectacular effects relies more on the skills of the stage technician than on the poet.

Now that we've established these principles, let's discuss how to properly structure a plot since this is the most important part of Tragedy.

As we defined it earlier, Tragedy is an imitation of an action that is complete, whole, and of a certain size. Something whole must have a beginning, a middle, and an end. A beginning is something that doesn't come after anything else by necessity but is followed by something naturally. An end is the opposite—it naturally follows something else, either by necessity or as a rule, but nothing follows after it. A middle is something that comes after one thing and is followed by another. A well-constructed plot shouldn't begin or end randomly but should follow these principles.

Also, a beautiful object, whether it's a living being or anything made up of parts, must not only have a well-organized arrangement of parts but also be of a certain size. Beauty depends on size and order. A very small living thing can't be beautiful because we can't see it clearly, and it's hard to understand in such a short amount of time. But something too large can't be beautiful either because we can't see it all at once, and the sense of its unity is lost for the viewer. For example, imagine something a thousand miles long. In the same way, a plot needs to be of a certain length that can be easily understood in one viewing. The specific limits of length for dramatic competition or stage performance aren't part of artistic theory. If the rule was to have a hundred tragedies compete at the same time, the performance would have to be controlled by a water clock, as we're told was once done. But the limit set by the nature of the drama is this: the longer the play, the more beautiful it can be because of its size, as long as it's still clear and easy to understand. To roughly define this, we can say that the proper size is within limits that allow the events to logically or necessarily change from bad fortune to good, or from good fortune to bad.

A plot's unity doesn't come from having just one hero, as some people think. A person's life can have many different events that can't be made into one unified story. Also, a person can do many different actions that don't form one single action. This is why the poets who wrote about Heracles, Theseus, or others made a mistake. They believed that because Heracles was one man, the story about him must also be unified. But Homer, as usual, seems to have seen the truth better than others, whether through skill or natural talent. When he wrote the Odyssey, he didn't include all of Odysseus's adventures, like the time he was wounded on Mount Parnassus or when he pretended to be mad to avoid going to war. These events weren't connected in a necessary or likely way. Instead, Homer made the Odyssey, like the Iliad, focus on one action, as we understand it. Just like in other imitative arts, the imitation is unified when the thing being imitated is one. So, the plot, being an imitation of an action, should imitate one complete action. The parts of the story should be connected so that if you remove or move one part, the whole story would fall apart. If something can be removed and nothing changes, then it's not really an essential part of the story.

It's clear from this that the poet's job isn't to tell us what has happened, but what could happen—what is possible according to what's likely or necessary. A poet and a historian don't differ by whether they write in verse or prose. You could take the work of Herodotus, put it into verse, and it would still be history, just with a meter. The real difference is that one tells what has happened, and the other tells what could happen. Poetry, then, is more philosophical and higher than history because poetry talks about the universal, while history talks about the specific. By "universal," I mean how certain types of people would probably act or speak in certain situations, according to what's likely or necessary. This is what poetry tries to show by giving names to its characters. The specific would be, for example, what Alcibiades did or experienced. We can already see this in Comedy: the poet first creates the plot based on what's likely, and then adds the characters' names, unlike those who write personal attacks focused on real people. Tragedians often still use real names, though, because things that could happen are easier to believe. If something hasn't happened, we might not believe it's possible right away, but if it has happened, we know it's possible—because it already did. Still, some tragedies use only one or two real names, with the rest being made up. In others, all the names are fictional, like in Agathon's Antheus, where both the events and the characters are made up, and yet the play is still enjoyable. So, we don't need to stick strictly to traditional stories, which are usually the subjects of tragedy. It would be silly to insist on this because even well-known stories are only known by a few people, but they still give pleasure to everyone.

This shows that the poet should focus on creating the plot rather than just writing verses because the poet's main job is to imitate, and what he imitates is actions. Even if he uses a historical subject, he's still a poet. There's no reason why actual events can't follow the laws of what's possible and likely, and if they do, he is still their poet.

The worst kind of plot is the episodic one. By "episodic," I mean a plot where the events follow one another without a logical or necessary connection. Bad poets create these by their own mistakes, while good poets sometimes do it to please the actors. Since they write for contests, they stretch the plot too far and end up breaking the natural flow of events.

But tragedy doesn't just imitate a complete action. It also imitates events that cause fear or pity. These emotions are best triggered when the events happen unexpectedly and are connected by cause and effect. The shock is even greater when it seems like there's a plan behind the events. For example, take the statue of Mitys in Argos. It fell on his murderer while he was watching a festival and killed him. These kinds of events don't seem like they happen by chance. So, plots that follow these principles are the best.

Plots can be either simple or complex, just like the actions in real life that they imitate. I call a plot simple when the change of fortune happens without a reversal or recognition. A complex plot is when the change comes with a reversal, recognition, or both. These should come naturally from the structure of the plot, so that what happens seems like the necessary or likely outcome of what came before. It's very important whether something happens because of something else or just after something else.

A reversal is when the situation suddenly changes into its opposite, always following the rules of probability or necessity. For example, in Oedipus, the messenger comes to cheer Oedipus up by easing his worries about his mother, but by revealing who Oedipus really is, he causes the opposite effect. Another example is in Lynceus. Lynceus is being taken away to be killed, and Danaus goes with him to kill him. But in the end, Danaus is killed, and Lynceus is saved.

Recognition, as the name suggests, is a change from ignorance to knowledge, which brings love or hate between the people destined by the poet for good or bad fortune. The best kind of recognition happens at the same time as a reversal, like in Oedipus. There are other types of recognition too. Even inanimate objects can sometimes be recognized, though in a less important way. We can also recognize whether someone has done something or not. But the most important kind of recognition, the one most tied to the plot, is the recognition of people. This kind of recognition, combined with a reversal, will create either pity or fear, and these are the emotions that tragedy aims to produce. The outcome of good or bad fortune depends on these moments of recognition. Recognition happens between people, and sometimes only one person recognizes the other while the other is already known. Other times, both must recognize each other. For example, Iphigenia is revealed to Orestes when she sends a letter, but another recognition is needed for Orestes to be revealed to Iphigenia.

So, two parts of the plot—reversal and recognition—depend on surprises. The third part is the scene of suffering. A scene of suffering is when something destructive or painful happens, like death, physical pain, wounds, or similar things.

Section 2

The parts of a Tragedy that need to be treated as the elements of the whole have already been mentioned. Now, we move on to the main parts—the individual sections into which a Tragedy is divided. These are the Prologue, Episode, Exode, and Choric Song, which itself is divided into the Parode and Stasimon. These are found in all plays, but some plays also have actor songs from the stage and the Commoi, which are unique to those plays.

The Prologue is the part of the Tragedy that comes before the Chorus enters with the Parode. The Episode is the part that comes between the choral songs. The Exode is the final part of the Tragedy, which has no choral song following it. The Parode is the first full song of the Chorus, and the Stasimon is a choral ode without anapaests or trochaic tetrameters. The Commos is a shared lament between the Chorus and the actors. These parts must all be treated as essential elements of the whole.

Now that we've covered these basics, we need to look at what the poet should aim for and what they should avoid when constructing their plots. We also need to consider how to create the specific emotional effects that Tragedy is meant to inspire.

As we've already seen, a perfect Tragedy should not follow a simple plan but rather a complex one. It should also imitate actions that make us feel pity and fear, as this is the hallmark of Tragedy. From this, it's clear that the change in fortune shown should not be a virtuous person going from good times to bad. This would neither inspire pity nor fear, only shock. Nor should it be a bad person going from bad times to good, as this has no place in Tragedy. It doesn't meet any of the tragic criteria and doesn't make us feel pity or fear. Nor should we see the downfall of a complete villain, as this might satisfy our moral sense but would not inspire pity or fear. Pity is felt for someone who experiences misfortune they don't deserve, and fear comes when we see someone like ourselves face misfortune. So, such an event would not be tragic.

Instead, the character should be someone between these extremes. He shouldn't be completely good or just, but his misfortune shouldn't come from being evil either. Instead, it should be due to some mistake or weakness. This person should also be someone of high status and success, like Oedipus, Thyestes, or other notable figures.

A well-made plot should therefore be single in its outcome, rather than double, as some suggest. The change in fortune should go from good to bad, not the other way around. It should happen not because of evil, but because of a great mistake or weakness in a character like the one we've described or someone even better. We can see this idea in practice on stage. In the beginning, poets would tell any story that came their way. But now, the best tragedies are based on the stories of a few families—like the tales of Alcmaeon, Oedipus, Orestes, Meleager, Thyestes, and Telephus—who have done or suffered something tragic. A perfect Tragedy, according to the rules of art, should be built this way. Therefore, those who criticize Euripides for ending many of his plays unhappily are mistaken. As we've said, this is the correct way to end a tragedy. The best proof of this is that in dramatic competitions, such plays, when well executed, are the most moving. Even though Euripides may not always handle his subjects perfectly, he is still considered the most tragic of the poets.

In second place comes a type of Tragedy that some people rank first. This type has a double plot, like the *Odyssey*, with one outcome for the good characters and another for the bad ones. Some people think this is the best type because of the audience's preferences. Poets often write based on what the audience wants. However, the pleasure from this type of Tragedy isn't the true pleasure of Tragedy. It's more suited to Comedy, where the deadliest enemies, like Orestes and Aegisthus, can leave the stage as friends, and no one kills or is killed.

Fear and pity can be created by spectacular effects, but they can also come from the plot itself, which is the better way and shows a more skilled poet. The plot should be arranged so that even without seeing it, just hearing the story would still make the listener feel horror and pity. This is the kind of response we get from hearing the story of *Oedipus*. But creating this effect through mere spectacle is a less artistic approach, relying on outside help. Those who use special effects to create something shocking, but not terrifying, miss the point of Tragedy. We shouldn't expect every kind of pleasure from Tragedy, only the kind that belongs to it. Since the pleasure a poet should aim for is that which comes from pity and fear through imitation, the plot must be built to create these feelings.

So, let's now think about what kinds of situations are most likely to make us feel fear or pity.

The events must happen between people who are either friends, enemies, or indifferent to one another.

If an enemy kills an enemy, neither the action nor the intention will make us feel pity, except for the suffering involved. The same goes for indifferent people. But when something tragic happens between people who are close or who care about each other—like a brother killing a brother, a son killing his father, or a mother killing her son—these are the kinds of situations the poet should focus on. The poet doesn't need to change the basic structure of the traditional stories—like the fact that Clytemnestra was killed by Orestes or Eriphyle by Alcmaeon—but they should skillfully handle the existing material. Let's explain what it means to handle it skillfully.

The action may be done knowingly, with full understanding of who the people are, as the older poets often wrote. For instance, Euripides has Medea kill her children this way. Or, the action may be done unknowingly, and only later does the person realize the connection, like in *Oedipus* by Sophocles. In *Oedipus*, the incident happens outside the main story, but there are other examples where the recognition happens within the plot, like in the *Alcmaeon* of Astydamas or when Telegonus wounds Odysseus. Another example is when someone is about to act with full knowledge but chooses not to. Finally, there's the case where someone is about to do something irreversible in ignorance but discovers the truth just in time. These are the only possible scenarios. The deed must either be done or not, and it can happen with or without knowledge. Of these, the worst is when someone is about to act with knowledge but doesn't. This is shocking without being tragic because no disaster happens. This approach is rarely found in poetry, though there's an example in *Antigone* when Haemon threatens to kill Creon. A better approach is for the deed to actually be done. Even better is when it's done in ignorance, and the truth is discovered afterward. This way, the recognition is surprising, but nothing too shocking happens. The best scenario is when someone is about to kill someone they don't recognize, but then recognizes them just in time. This happens in *Cresphontes*, where Merope almost kills her son but recognizes him in time. In *Iphigenia*, the sister recognizes her brother just before she's about to harm him. Similarly, in *Helle*, the son recognizes his mother just before turning her in. This is why only a few families provide the subjects for most tragedies. It wasn't skill but luck that led poets to these stories, which naturally lend themselves to tragedy.

We've now covered enough about how the plot should be structured and the right kind of plot for a Tragedy.

When it comes to characters, there are four key things to aim for. First and most importantly, the character must be good. Any speech or action that shows moral purpose will reveal character, and the character will be good if the purpose is good. This rule applies to all types of people. Even women and slaves can have good character, though women were seen as weaker, and slaves were considered unimportant. The second thing to aim for is propriety. There is a type of courage that's proper for a man, but it wouldn't be fitting for a woman to show the same kind of courage. The third goal is for the character to be realistic. This is different from the idea of being good or proper. The fourth goal is consistency. Even if the character being imitated is inconsistent, they should be consistently inconsistent. For example, in *Orestes*, Menelaus' character lacks purpose, while in *Scylla*, the lament of Odysseus is inappropriate. In *Iphigenia at Aulis*, the character is inconsistent, as the Iphigenia who begs for her life is very different from her later self.

Just like with the plot, the poet should aim for what is necessary or probable when portraying characters. A person of a certain type should speak or act in a certain way, following the rules of necessity or probability. In the same way, one event should follow another in a necessary or probable sequence. It's clear, then, that the resolution of the plot, like its complications, should come from within the plot itself. It shouldn't rely on the *Deus ex Machina*, as in *Medea* or the return of the Greeks in the *Iliad*.

The *Deus ex Machina* should only be used for events that happen outside the main story, events that are beyond human knowledge and need to be reported or predicted. We believe the gods have the power to see everything. But within the action of the play, nothing irrational should happen. If something irrational can't be avoided, it should occur outside the Tragedy. One example of this is in *Oedipus* by Sophocles.

Since Tragedy imitates people who are above the common level, poets should follow the example of good portrait painters. These painters capture the true likeness of their subjects but also make them look more beautiful. In the same way, poets, when representing characters with flaws like anger or laziness, should maintain the character's type while also ennobling them. This is how Achilles is portrayed by Agathon and Homer.

These are the rules a poet should follow. They also shouldn't ignore the emotional appeals that, while not essential, are part of poetry. There is much room for error in this area, but we've already said enough about this in our earlier discussions.

Recognition has already been explained, but now we will go over the different types.

The least artistic form of recognition is the one most commonly used, which is recognition by signs. Some of these signs are natural, like "the spear that the earth-born race carries on their bodies," or the stars mentioned by Carcinus in his *Thyestes*. Others are acquired after birth, like scars, or external tokens, like necklaces or the little chest in *Tyro*, which helps reveal a character. Even these can be used more or less skillfully. For example, in *The Odyssey*, Odysseus is recognized by his scar, but the discovery is made in one way by the nurse and in another way by the swineherds. The use of signs for proof, or any formal proof, whether with or without tokens, is less artistic. A better form of recognition is when it happens through a turn of events, like in the bath scene in *The Odyssey*.

Next is the type of recognition that is simply created by the poet, and this is not very artistic because it doesn't feel natural. For example, in *Iphigenia*, Orestes reveals that he is Orestes. Iphigenia makes herself known by showing a letter, but Orestes just says who he is without it being required by the plot. This is similar to the fault mentioned before— Orestes could have just as easily brought a sign or token with him. Another example is the "voice of the shuttle" in Sophocles' *Tereus*.

The third type of recognition happens through memory, when the sight of an object stirs an emotional response. An example is in *The Cyprians* by Dicaeogenes, where the hero breaks down in tears upon seeing a picture. Another example is in *The Lay of Alcinous*, where Odysseus hears the minstrel play the lyre and remembers his past, which causes him to weep, leading to recognition.

The fourth kind is recognition through reasoning. For instance, in *The Choephori*: "Someone like me has arrived. No one looks like me except Orestes, so Orestes must be here." Another example is in *Iphigenia* by Polyidus, where Orestes reflects, "So I, too, must die at the altar like my sister." In *Tydeus* by Theodectes, the father says, "I came to find my son, but I am losing my own life." And in *The Phineidae*, the women see the place and deduce their fate: "Here we are doomed to die, for here we were abandoned." There's also a type of recognition that involves a false conclusion, like in *Odysseus Disguised as a Messenger*. One character mistakenly believes that another will recognize a bow, even though that person has never seen it, and this false assumption leads to recognition.

However, the best type of recognition is the one that arises naturally from the events in the story. This happens when the recognition is part of the unfolding action, as in *Oedipus* by Sophocles, or in *Iphigenia*, where it makes sense that Iphigenia would want to send a letter. These recognitions don't need the artificial help of tokens or signs. After this, the next best kind is recognition through reasoning.

When writing a plot and deciding on the language, the poet should imagine the scene as clearly as possible. By picturing everything vividly, as if they were watching it happen, the poet will better understand what fits the situation and avoid inconsistencies. The need for this rule is shown by the mistake made by Carcinus. In his play, Amphiaraus was coming from the temple, but the audience found it unbelievable because the playwright didn't envision the situation properly. As a result, the play failed because the audience noticed this mistake.

The poet should also write their play with the right actions in mind. When a character feels an emotion, they should show it convincingly through their actions. For example, someone who is agitated should storm around, and someone who is angry should rage, all in a lifelike way. This is why poetry requires either a natural talent or a touch of madness. In the first case, the poet can step into the character's shoes, and in the second, they can lose themselves in the role.

As for the plot, whether the poet takes it from an existing story or creates it themselves, they should first outline the general idea and then fill in the details and episodes. A good example of this is *Iphigenia*.

The basic plot is that a young girl is sacrificed and disappears mysteriously. She is transported to a foreign land where the custom is to sacrifice strangers to the goddess. She becomes part of this ritual. Later, her brother arrives, having been sent there by an oracle. He is captured and almost sacrificed, but then reveals who he is. The recognition could happen in the way Euripides wrote it, or as Polyidus imagined, where the brother says, "So it's not just my sister who was supposed to be sacrificed, but me too." This realization saves him.

Once the general plot is clear, the poet must ensure that the episodes are relevant to the action. In the case of Orestes, for example, there is the madness that leads to his capture, followed by his rescue through a purification ritual. In drama, the episodes are usually short, but in epic poetry, they are what extend the story. For example, the basic plot of *The Odyssey* can be summed up simply: a man is away from home for many years, while his home is plagued by suitors who waste his wealth and plot against his son. Finally, after many struggles, he returns home, reveals his identity to certain people, kills the suitors, and restores order. This is the core of the story, and everything else is just additional episodes.

Every tragedy has two main parts: the Complication and the Unraveling, or Denouement. The Complication includes everything from the beginning of the play until the turning point where the action changes to either good or bad fortune. The Unraveling covers everything from the turning point to the end of the play. For example, in *Lynceus* by Theodectes, the Complication includes the events leading up to the child's capture, and the Unraveling starts with the accusation of murder and continues to the end.

There are four types of tragedy: the Complex, which relies heavily on Reversals of the Situation and Recognition; the Pathetic, where the main motive is passion, like in the tragedies about Ajax and Ixion; the Ethical, where the motivation is moral, like in *Phthiotides* and *Peleus*; and the Simple. Spectacular tragedies, like *Phorcides* or *Prometheus*, rely more on visual elements. A poet should try to combine as many elements of these types as possible, or at least the most important ones, especially considering modern criticism. While past poets excelled in specific areas, today's critics expect one poet to master them all.

When determining whether two tragedies are the same or different, the best way to judge is by looking at the plot. If the Complication and the Unraveling are the same, then the tragedies are considered the same. Many poets are good at creating a strong beginning but struggle to resolve the story. Both skills are necessary, and the poet should master them.

The poet should also avoid turning an epic into a tragedy. By "epic," I mean a story with many plots, like trying to make a tragedy out of the entire *Iliad*. In an epic, each part of the story has room to develop, but in a tragedy, this would not work as well. The best example of this mistake is when poets have tried to dramatize the entire story of the Fall of Troy instead of just selecting certain parts, as Euripides did. Similarly, poets who try to tell the whole story of *Niobe*, instead of focusing on just part of it, fail on stage. Even Agathon has made this mistake. However, Agathon shows great skill in his Reversals of the Situation, trying to please the audience by creating a tragic effect that satisfies their moral sense. This happens when a clever villain, like Sisyphus, is outwitted, or a brave villain is defeated. These outcomes are considered probable in Agathon's view, who argues that "many things happen against probability."

The Chorus should be seen as one of the actors. It should be an integral part of the story and share in the action, more like how Sophocles used the Chorus rather than Euripides. In contrast, later poets often write choral songs that have little to do with the main story, turning them into mere interludes. This practice was first started by Agathon. But there's little difference between adding choral interludes and bringing in a speech or even an entire act from another play.

We have already discussed most parts of Tragedy, but now we need to talk about Diction and Thought. For Thought, we can refer to what has been said in *Rhetoric*, since this subject fits better under that area of study. Thought includes anything that speech is supposed to accomplish. These can be things like proving or disproving something, stirring emotions like pity, fear, or anger, or suggesting something is important or not. It's clear that dramatic incidents must be handled the same way as speeches when the goal is to create feelings of pity, fear, importance, or probability. The main difference is that the incidents should show these effects on their own, without needing to be explained in words, while the effects in speeches must come from what the speaker says. After all, what would be the point of speaking if the meaning was already clear without it?

Now, let's talk about Diction. One part of this subject deals with different types of speech. However, this is more related to the art of delivery, which is something taught by specialists in that field. It includes things like knowing what counts as a command, a prayer, a statement, a threat, a question, or an answer. Whether or not someone understands these things isn't a big deal for the art of poetry itself. For example, Protagoras criticized Homer, saying that when

Homer wrote, "Sing, goddess, of the wrath," he was giving a command when he thought he was making a request. But to ask someone to do something or not do something is, Protagoras said, a command. We can set this issue aside, though, because it belongs to another field, not poetry.

Language as a whole can be broken down into different parts: Letters, Syllables, Connecting Words, Nouns, Verbs, Inflections (or Cases), and Sentences (or Phrases).

A *Letter* is a sound that can't be broken down into smaller sounds, but not just any sound, because even animals make sounds that can't be divided. But those aren't letters. The sound must be something that can be part of a group of sounds, and letters can be vowels, semivowels, or mutes. A vowel is a sound you can hear clearly without using your tongue or lips, like "A" or "E." A semivowel is a sound that requires some contact with your tongue or lips, like "S" or "R." A mute is a sound that, by itself, doesn't make any noise, but when combined with a vowel, it becomes audible, like "G" or "D." These letters are distinguished by how the mouth is shaped when they're pronounced and where in the mouth they are formed. They can be pronounced in different ways, like being aspirated or smooth, long or short, or pronounced with a high, low, or medium tone. All of this is something studied by people who specialize in meter.

A *Syllable* is a combination of a mute and a vowel, but it doesn't mean anything on its own. For example, "GR" without the "A" is a syllable, and "GRA" with the "A" is also a syllable. These distinctions are also studied in metrical science.

A *Connecting Word* is a sound that doesn't mean anything by itself but connects or separates other sounds that do have meaning. It can appear at the beginning, middle, or end of a sentence. It could be a word like "and" or "but," which helps join several significant words into one meaningful unit, or it might simply indicate the start, end, or division of a sentence. Some words, however, can't stand on their own at the beginning of a sentence, such as "men," "etoi," or "de."

A *Noun* is a meaningful sound made up of smaller parts that, on their own, don't carry any meaning. For example, in the compound word *Theodorus*, which means "god-given," the parts "theos" (god) and "doron" (gift) don't have the same significance when they're separated.

A *Verb* is also a meaningful sound made up of smaller parts, but unlike a noun, it indicates time. For example, "man" or "white" doesn't suggest any time frame, but "he walks" or "he has walked" includes an idea of when the action takes place—whether it's present or past.

Inflection applies to both nouns and verbs and shows relationships like possession ("of" or "to"), or number, whether singular or plural (like "man" or "men"). Inflection can also indicate how something is said, whether as a question or a command. For example, "Did he go?" and "Go!" show different verbal inflections.

A *Sentence* or *Phrase* is a group of words that together form a meaningful unit, with at least some parts that are meaningful on their own. Not every sentence needs verbs and nouns. For example, "the definition of man" doesn't need a verb but still makes sense. Sentences will always have some part that is meaningful, like "in walking" or "Cleon, son of Cleon." A sentence can be considered a single unit in two ways: either because it expresses one idea or because it links several parts together. For example, *The Iliad* is a whole because its parts are connected, and "the definition of man" is whole because it expresses one single idea.

· · ·

Section 3

Words can be either simple or compound. A simple word is made of parts that don't mean anything by themselves, like "ge" meaning "earth." A compound word is made up of either one meaningful and one non-meaningful part, or two parts that both mean something. Some words can even be triple, quadruple, or even longer, like certain expressions from Massilia, such as "Hermo-caico-xanthus" [who prayed to Father Zeus].

Every word can be classified as either common, unusual, metaphorical, decorative, newly-coined, lengthened, shortened, or changed.

A common word is one that everyone in a certain place uses. An unusual word is one used in a different country. So, the same word can be both common and unusual, but not for the same group of people. For example, the word sigynon, meaning "lance," is common for people in Cyprus, but unusual for us.

A metaphor is when you use a word from one thing to describe something else. This can happen in a few ways: from a general term to a more specific one, from a specific term to a more general one, from one specific thing to another specific thing, or by comparing things that are similar in some way. For example, when someone says, "There lies my ship," the idea of lying is transferred from a general meaning (like lying down) to something more specific (the ship lying at anchor). Another example is saying, "Odysseus has performed ten thousand great deeds." Here, the specific number "ten thousand" is used to mean a large number in general. You can also compare two specific things, like saying, "He drew out the life with a blade of bronze," meaning he killed someone with a sword, or "He cut the water with a bronze vessel," meaning he steered a ship through water. These are examples of taking one action and using it to describe another similar action.

Another type of metaphor is analogy, where one thing relates to another in the same way a third thing relates to a fourth. For example, a cup relates to Dionysus (the god of wine) in the same way a shield relates to Ares (the god of war). So, you could call a cup "the shield of Dionysus" or a shield "the cup of Ares." Another example is comparing old age to life and evening to the day. So, we might say "evening

50

is the old age of the day" or "old age is the evening of life." Some analogies work even if we don't have a specific word for them. For instance, there's no word for the way the sun "sows" its light like a farmer sows seeds. But poets can still use the phrase "sowing light" to describe the sun.

A newly-coined word is one that the poet creates for the first time, like calling horns "sprouters" or a priest "a supplicator."

A word is lengthened when a vowel is replaced by a longer one, or when a syllable is added. A word is shortened when part of it is removed. An example of lengthening would be saying "poleos" instead of "poles," or "Peleiadeo" instead of "Peleidou." An example of shortening would be words like "kri" for "krisis" or "do" for "doma."

An altered word is when part of the word stays the same, but another part is changed. For example, "dexiteron" is a modified version of "dexion," meaning "on the right side."

Nouns can be masculine, feminine, or neuter. Masculine nouns end in N, R, S, or letters combined with S, like PS and X. Feminine nouns end in vowels that are always long, like E and O, and sometimes A when it can be lengthened. The total number of letters in masculine and feminine nouns is the same because PS and X count as S endings. No noun ends with a mute sound or a naturally short vowel. Only three nouns end in I: meli (honey), kommi (gum), and peperi (pepper). Five nouns end in U, and neuter nouns can end in I, U, N, or S.

The best style is clear without being too plain. A clear style uses common words, but it can sound simple or boring, as seen in the poetry of Cleophon and Sthenelus. On the other hand, a more sophisticated style uses unusual words. By "unusual," I mean words that are rare, metaphorical, or lengthened in some way that makes them different from everyday language. However, if a style is filled with nothing but these types of words, it becomes either a riddle or confusing gibberish. It's a riddle if it's filled with metaphors, and it becomes gibberish if it's filled with rare words. A riddle expresses true ideas through unexpected combinations of words, something that can't be done with ordinary speech but is possible with metaphors. For example, "I saw a man glue bronze onto another man using fire" is a metaphorical riddle. A style full of rare words sounds like nonsense. Therefore, a good style should have a mix of these elements. The unusual words, metaphors, and decorative language will make it sound elevated, while common words will keep it clear.

Nothing contributes more to making a style sound fresh and interesting than using lengthened, shortened, or altered words. If a writer sometimes breaks from the usual language in small ways, it gives the style a special quality, but keeping some of the usual forms ensures clarity. Some critics make the mistake of mocking these language changes. For example, Eucleides, an older critic, claimed it was easy to be a poet if you could just lengthen syllables however you liked. He exaggerated this practice to make fun of it, saying things like, "I saw Epichares walking to Marathon" or "Not if you want his hellebore." Overusing this kind of change can sound silly, but when used properly, it can enhance poetic language. Even metaphors and rare words can seem ridiculous if used without care or if the goal is to be funny.

A great example of how word choice can change the tone is in Epic poetry. If you replace unusual words or metaphors with more common terms, you can see how it affects the beauty of the line. For instance, both Aeschylus and Euripides wrote a line with the same basic meaning, but Euripides used a rarer word, which made his version seem more elegant. Aeschylus wrote, "The tumor eats away the flesh of my foot," while Euripides changed "eats" to "feasts on," making the line sound more powerful.

It's important to use all these types of words appropriately. Metaphors, compound words, and unusual terms can give style a higher quality, but using them poorly makes the writing sound strange. Above all, having a talent for using metaphors is the greatest skill. This can't be taught—it's a sign of natural genius because it requires seeing connections between things.

Different kinds of words work better for different types of poetry. Compound words are best for songs, rare words are suited for heroic poetry, and metaphors fit iambic verse. In heroic poetry, you can use all these types, but in iambic verse, which is closer to everyday speech, it's better to use more familiar words, including common words, metaphors, and decorative language.

This concludes the discussion of Tragedy and how it imitates action.

When it comes to poetic works that are written in a narrative style and use a single meter, the plot should be built the same way as a tragedy. It should focus on one main action, complete with a beginning, middle, and end. This gives the poem unity, like a living organism, and provides the right kind of pleasure. This is different from historical writings, which don't focus on a single action but instead cover everything that happened within a specific time period to one or many people, even if those events aren't closely connected. For example, the sea battle at Salamis and the battle with the Carthaginians in Sicily happened at the same time but didn't lead to the same result. Events sometimes follow one another without leading to a single outcome. This is how most poets handle their stories.

Once again, we can see Homer's exceptional skill. He didn't try to make the entire Trojan War the subject of his poem, even though the war had a clear beginning and end. That would have been too large a subject to handle in one work. If Homer had tried to limit it to a more manageable size, the story would have become overly complicated due to all the different events. Instead, he chose to focus on just one part of the war and included other events as episodes, like the Catalogue of the Ships, to add variety to the poem. Other poets take a different approach by focusing on one hero, one time period, or one action, but these often have too many parts. This is what the authors of The Cypria and The Little Iliad did. That's why The Iliad and The Odyssey are each the subject of just one or two tragedies, while The Cypria is used for many tragedies and The Little Iliad is used for eight.

Epic poetry, like Tragedy, can be simple, complex, focused on character, or focused on emotion. The elements, except for song and spectacle, are the same. Epics also use Reversals of the Situation, Recognitions, and Scenes of Suffering. The thoughts and diction (language) must be artistic. Homer is the best model for this, as his poems excel in both diction and thought. The Iliad is both simple and focused on emotion, while The Odyssey is complex, with many recognition scenes, and it also has a strong focus on character. In both cases, Homer's language and ideas are outstanding.

Epic poetry is different from Tragedy because it is longer and uses a different meter. We have already set a reasonable length limit: the beginning and end should fit into a single view. This can be achieved with shorter poems than the old epics, similar to the length of a group of tragedies presented in one sitting.

However, epic poetry has a special ability to be longer and still work well, and the reason for this is clear. In Tragedy, we can't show multiple events happening at the same time; we have to focus on what is happening on stage with the characters. But in Epic poetry, because it's told in a narrative style, many events can be presented as happening at the same time. As long as these events are connected to the main story, they make the poem more impressive and grand. This is an advantage of epics, as it helps create a sense of grandeur and keeps the audience interested with varied episodes. In contrast, when a tragedy's events become repetitive, it quickly becomes boring and loses its effect.

As for the meter, the heroic hexameter has proven to be the best. If a narrative poem were written in any other meter or mixed meters, it would feel out of place. The heroic meter is the grandest and most serious, and it easily allows for the use of rare words and metaphors, which is another reason why this form of poetry stands out. On the other hand, the iambic and trochaic meters are more lively—one is closer to the rhythms of everyday speech, and the other is associated with dancing. It would be even more strange to mix different meters together, as Chaeremon once did. That's why no one has ever successfully written a large-scale poem in anything other than heroic verse. Nature itself, as we've mentioned, leads poets to choose this meter.

Homer is excellent in every way, but one of his greatest strengths is that he understands how much the poet should insert themselves into the story. The poet should speak as little as possible in their own voice because that doesn't count as imitation. Other poets constantly appear in their own works and don't focus much on imitating others. Homer, on the other hand, after a short introduction, brings in his characters—men, women, and others—each with their own distinct traits.

The element of the wonderful is important in Tragedy, but the irrational, which is often the source of wonder, has more freedom in Epic poetry because the person acting isn't seen. For example, the scene where Achilles chases Hector would look ridiculous on stage—the Greeks standing still while Achilles waves them back from joining the chase. But in an epic poem, this seems fine. The wonderful is enjoyable because people like to hear stories that stretch the truth. Homer was especially skilled at making up stories in a believable way. The trick lies in a kind of logical trick. If one thing happens or is true, we assume the next thing must be true as well. But sometimes, even if the second thing is true, the first isn't. Still, because our minds know the second part is true, we assume the first part is as well. Homer uses this trick in the bath scene of The Odyssey.

So, poets should aim for things that are improbable but still possible, rather than things that are possible but seem unlikely. The plot of a tragedy should avoid irrational events whenever possible. If there is something irrational, it should happen outside the main action of the play. For example, in Oedipus, the fact that the hero doesn't know how Laius was killed happens offstage. But in Electra, when the messenger describes the Pythian games, or in The Mysians, when a man travels from Tegea to Mysia and remains silent, the irrational is part of the main plot, which weakens it. The excuse that the plot would fall apart without these irrational parts is not valid. The plot should not have been built that way in the first place. However, once the irrational has been introduced and made believable, we must accept it. Even the impossible events in The Odyssey, like Odysseus being left on the shore of Ithaca, are acceptable because Homer handles them so well. A less skilled poet would have made these moments feel absurd.

The language of a poem should be carefully worked out during parts where there is no intense expression of character or thought. When characters are expressing deep emotions or ideas, using overly fancy language can obscure the meaning.

When facing difficulties or criticism about a poem, there are several ways to address the concerns.

A poet, like a painter or any other artist, must imitate one of three things: things as they were or are, things as people say or think they are, or things as they should be. The poet uses language—either common words, rare words, or metaphors. We also allow poets to use certain modifications of language that we wouldn't accept in everyday speech. What's considered "correct" in poetry isn't the same as in politics or other fields. Within poetry, there are two kinds of mistakes: those that affect the essence of the work and those that are just minor details. If a poet tries to imitate something but does it badly, the error is fundamental. But if the poet makes a mistake in the choice of subject—like showing a horse moving in an impossible way or using incorrect medical facts—these are minor errors. This is how we should address criticisms of a poet's work.

When the poet includes something impossible, it's a mistake, but it might be excused if it helps achieve the poem's goal. The goal, as mentioned earlier, is to create an emotional impact. For example, the pursuit of Hector in The Iliad works because it makes the scene more dramatic, even if it's not realistic. But if the same effect could have been achieved without breaking the rules of poetry, then the mistake is not justified. We should avoid errors whenever possible.

It's also important to ask whether the mistake affects the core of the poem or just a minor detail. For example, not knowing that deer don't have horns is a smaller mistake than depicting the animal poorly.

If someone argues that something isn't realistic, the poet can respond by saying, "But that's how it should be." Sophocles famously said he portrayed people as they should be, while Euripides showed them as they are. This response works if the scene reflects an ideal version of reality. If it doesn't, the poet might argue, "This is how people say it happened," especially in stories about the gods. Even if the stories are not higher than reality or strictly true, as Xenophanes pointed out, they are at least what people say. Sometimes, the poet can simply point out that the event really happened. For example, in The Iliad, the poet says, "The spears stood upright on their butts." This might sound strange, but it was the custom at the time, and it's still done by the Illyrians today.

When we judge whether something said or done in a poem is right, we shouldn't only look at the action itself. We also need to consider who did it, to whom it was done, when it happened, how it was done, and why it was done. For example, we should ask whether the action was done to achieve a greater good or avoid a worse evil.

Some difficulties can be solved by looking at how language is used. For example, in the phrase "the mules first [he killed]," the poet might have used the word "mules" to mean "guards" instead. Or, in the description of Dolon, when the poet says he was "ill-favored," it doesn't mean his body was poorly shaped but that his face was ugly. In Crete, the word for "well-favored" refers to a beautiful face.

Sometimes, an expression is metaphorical. For example, when the poet says, "All gods and men were sleeping through the night," he later mentions that some people were awake and playing music.

Here, "all" is used metaphorically to mean "many," since "all" is a kind of "many." Similarly, in the line "alone she had no part," the word "alone" is also metaphorical, meaning that she was the most famous.

Other solutions might come from how the sentence is punctuated. In some cases, changing the punctuation clears up any confusion. For example, in the lines from Empedocles: "Things that had been immortal suddenly became mortal, and things unmixed became mixed."

In some cases, the meaning changes based on how a word is used. For example, in the phrase "the night passed," the word "passed" has more than one meaning.

Or, a word might be used in a general way. For instance, any kind of mixed drink is called "wine," so Ganymede is said to serve wine to Zeus, even though the gods don't drink wine. The same applies to calling ironworkers "bronze-workers," which could also be seen as a metaphor.

Sometimes, when a word seems to have conflicting meanings, we need to think about how many ways it can be interpreted in that context. For example, in the phrase "the spear was checked there," we should ask what exactly "checked" means. Critics often make assumptions and then criticize based on those assumptions, but we should always examine what the poet actually said.

One example is the story about Icarius. Some critics assume he was from Sparta, so they find it strange that Telemachus didn't meet him when he visited Sparta. But according to another version of the story, Icarius was from Cephallenia, and Odysseus married a local woman. The critics' objection is based on a simple mistake.

In general, anything impossible in the story must be justified either by the needs of the plot, by aiming for a higher truth, or by accepted beliefs. When it comes to the needs of the plot, something impossible but believable is better than something possible but unlikely. For example, it might be impossible for people like Zeuxis' paintings to exist, but we accept it because the ideal is meant to surpass reality. If something irrational is included, we can justify it by saying that it's based on what people commonly say. Even irrational things can seem reasonable at times, like when something happens that seems impossible but is still believable.

When something seems contradictory, we should examine it the same way we would in a logical argument: by asking whether the same thing is being described, in the same way, and in the same sense. We should resolve questions by referring to what the poet actually says or what an intelligent person would understand to be implied.

The inclusion of irrational events or immoral characters should be criticized when there's no good reason for it. This is true of the irrational part of Euripides' introduction of Aegeus and the negative portrayal of Menelaus in Orestes.

In summary, there are five main types of objections critics raise: things that are impossible, irrational, harmful, contradictory, or artistically incorrect. The answers to these objections should be found using the ideas we've discussed.

The question might be asked: is Epic poetry or Tragedy the higher form of imitation? If we agree that the higher form of art is the one that appeals to a more refined audience, then the art that imitates anything and everything would clearly be less refined. This is because it assumes the audience is too simple to understand unless the performers add something extra, like exaggerated movements. Poor flute-players, for example, twist and spin around when they try to imitate "the quoit-throw," or they push around the chorus leader when performing Scylla. People claim that Tragedy has the same problem. We can compare this to how older actors viewed their younger counterparts. Mynniscus called Callippides "an ape" because of his wild gestures, and people thought the same of Pindarus. In this way, Tragedy as a whole is seen as being like the younger actors, compared to Epic poetry, which is like the older, more experienced actors. Epic poetry, they say, is meant for a more cultured audience, who don't need exaggerated movements, while Tragedy is for a less refined crowd. So, since it's considered less refined, Tragedy is thought to be the lower of the two.

First of all, this criticism doesn't apply to the art of poetry itself but to acting. Gestures can be overdone just as much in the performance of Epic poetry as in Tragedy, as we see with people like Sosistratus in reciting epics or Mnasitheus the Opuntian in lyrical competitions. Secondly, not all action should be criticized, just as not all dancing is bad. It's only bad performances that deserve criticism, like the fault found in Callippides and others who are criticized for playing disgraceful women. Besides, Tragedy, like Epic poetry, can be effective even without acting. It shows its power just by being read. If Tragedy is better in every other way, then this issue isn't a real flaw.

Tragedy is better because it includes all the elements of Epic poetry, and it can even use the same meter, but it also adds music and visual effects, which provide even more pleasure. Tragedy also has a stronger impact whether it's being read or performed. Additionally, Tragedy reaches its goal in a shorter amount of time, which is more enjoyable than something that drags on and becomes watered down. For example, think about how different Sophocles' Oedipus would be if it were as long as The Iliad.

Also, Epic poetry tends to have less unity, as we can see by the fact that any Epic poem could be divided into several tragedies. If the story a poet chooses is unified and concise, it might feel cut short, but if it follows the Epic tradition of being long, it can end up feeling weak and drawn out. This happens when the poem is made up of many actions, like The Iliad and The Odyssey, which contain many parts, each with its own significance. Even so, these epics are as well-structured as possible and do a great job of imitating a single action.

If Tragedy is better than Epic poetry in all these ways, and also does a better job at fulfilling its purpose—since every art form should aim to create the kind of pleasure that's specific to it—it clearly follows that Tragedy is the higher form of art because it achieves its goal more perfectly.

This should be enough to explain the overall comparison between Tragedy and Epic poetry, their different kinds and parts, how many parts each has, what makes them good or bad, the criticisms they face, and the answers to those criticisms.

The End

Thank you for Reading

You've Just Read a Piece of the Greatest Library Ever Rebuilt

Thank you for reading.

This book is one of thousands we're restoring, reimagining, and translating as part of the **Modern Library of Alexandria** — a global movement to preserve and share humanity's most important ideas.

What was once lost to fire and time is now rising again — not just as memory, but as living, breathing knowledge, freely accessible to all.

What You Can Do Next:

- **Keep Reading.**

  Discover more legendary works — in beautiful print, audiobook, or digital form — at LibraryofAlexandria.com.

- **Build Your Own Library.**

  Every title is available as a paperback, hardcover, or collectible boxset — at true printing cost. Craft a personal library worthy of display.

- **Spread the Light.**

  Share this book. Tell others about the movement. Help us translate every timeless work into every language, so no reader is ever left behind.

By finishing this book, you've already taken part in something extraordinary.

Join us at LibraryofAlexandria.com

Together, we're rebuilding the greatest library the world has ever known.

With appreciation,
The Modern Library of Alexandria Team

Visit:

www.libraryofalexandria.com

Or scan the code below:

www.ingramcontent.com/pod-product-compliance
Lightning Source LLC
Chambersburg PA
CBHW010732270326
41934CB00016B/3461